Books are to be returned on or before
the last date below.

27. MAR. 2007

LIBREX —

weblinks

You don't need a computer to use this book. But, for readers who do have access to the Internet, the book provides links to recommended websites which offer additional information and resources on the subject.

You will find weblinks boxes like this on some pages of the book.

weblinks

For more information on improved fuel efficiency of cars, go to www.waylinks.co.uk/series/21debates/transportation

waylinks.co.uk

To help you find the recommended websites easily and quickly, weblinks are provided on our own website, **waylinks.co.uk**. These take you straight to the relevant websites and save you typing in the Internet address yourself.

Internet safety

↗ Never give out personal details, which include: your name, address, school, telephone number, email address, password and mobile number.

↗ Do not respond to messages which make you feel uncomfortable – tell an adult.

↗ Do not arrange to meet in person someone you have met on the Internet.

↗ Never send your picture or anything else to an online friend without a parent's or teacher's permission.

↗ If you see anything that worries you, tell an adult.

A note to adults
Internet use by children should be supervised. We recommend that you install filtering software which blocks unsuitable material.

Website content

The weblinks for this book are checked and updated regularly. However, because of the nature of the Internet, the content of a website may change at any time, or a website may close down without notice. While the Publishers regret any inconvenience this may cause readers, they cannot be responsible for the content of any website other than their own.

HODDER
Wayland

21ST CENTURY DEBATES

TRANSPORTATION
OUR IMPACT ON THE PLANET

ROB BOWDEN

HODDER
Wayland

an imprint of Hodder Children's Books

21st Century Debates Series

Genetics • Surveillance • Internet • Media • Artificial Intelligence • Climate Change • Energy • Rainforests • Waste, Recycling and Reuse • Endangered Species • Air Pollution • An Overcrowded World? • Food Supply • Water Supply • World Health • Global Debt • New Religious Movements • The Drugs Trade • Terrorism • Racism • Violence in Society • Tourism • Globalisation

Produced for Hodder Wayland by White-Thomson Publishing Ltd,
2/3 St Andrew's Place, Lewes, East Sussex BN7 1UP

Published in Great Britain in 2004 by Hodder Wayland, an imprint of Hodder Children's Books.

Project editor: Kelly Davis
Commissioning editor: Steve White-Thomson
Proofreader: David C. Sills, Proof Positive Reading Service
Series and book design: Chris Halls, Mind's Eye Design Ltd, Lewes
Picture research: Shelley Noronha, Glass Onion Pictures
Bar chart: Nick Hawken

Every effort has been made to trace copyright holders. However, the publishers apologize for any unintentional omissions and would be pleased in such cases to add an acknowledgment in any future editions.

British Library Cataloguing in Publication Data
Bowden, Rob
    Transportation. - (21st Century Debates)
    1. Transportation - Environmental aspects - Juvenile literature
    I. Title
    388
ISBN: 0 7502 3951 4

Printed in Hong Kong

Hodder Children's Books, a division of Hodder Headline Limited, 338 Euston Road, London NW1 3BH

Picture acknowledgements: Ballard Power Systems 21; EASI-Images 24, 29 and 51 (Rob Bowden); Chris Fairclough Photography 16, 22, 27, 30, 46, 47; HWPL 8 (Paul Kenward), 9, 10, 20 (Rolando Pujol), 36; Popperfoto 7 (Fabrizio Bensch), 12, 13 (Ian Hodgson), 23 (Larry Chan); Rex Features 25, 39, 48, 58; Still Pictures 14 (NRSC), 17 (Dylan Garcia), 18 (Mark Edwards), 31 (Thomas Raupach), 50 (John Maier), 52 (Alex S. Maclean), 53 (Martin Bond); Topham 37, 42, 44, 57; Travel Ink 32 (Allan Hartley), 35 (Derek Allan); WTPix 4, 6, 11, 28, 33 and cover foreground, 41, 43, 49 and cover background, 54, 55.

Cover: foreground picture shows a light rail system in Sydney, Australia; background picture shows safe storage for bicycles in Ravenna, Italy.

CONTENTS

A WORLD ON THE MOVE

'Transport has become a mainstream issue and has a fundamental impact on people's lives in both positive and negative ways.'

Transport 2000, UK

Stop to think!

If you were to step outside your home or school and stand still, even for a minute, you would notice that the world around you was on the move. You might see a pedestrian or cyclist pass by, or cars, buses and lorries on the roads. You might be able to hear a train on a nearby line or see an aeroplane

Whether by foot, bicycle, motorbike, car or bus, people and goods are constantly on the move at this busy road junction in Bangalore, India.

flying overhead. The fact is that people and goods are moving all around us, twenty-four hours a day. We are so accustomed to this movement that many of us give it relatively little thought, and yet there are many reasons why we should.

The benefits of mobility

Movement, or mobility, is not a problem. The mobility of people and goods is essential to the functioning of a country's economy. How, for example, would a city manage without its daily flow of commuting workers, or a factory without its delivery of raw materials and despatch of finished goods? Where mobility is hampered, economies can suffer, as in parts of Africa and Asia. There, poor transport infrastructure (roads, railways, etc) deters businesses from investing in the local economy as it makes it harder, and often more costly, to move goods and people around.

Mobility is also socially important. It brings people together to meet, discuss, trade, relax and enjoy leisure pursuits. It also gives people greater personal freedom, such as the ability to travel and enjoy new experiences. These benefits are seen by many people in wealthier, more developed countries as basic rights, and any threat to personal mobility is taken very seriously.

The costs of mobility

Unfortunately the benefits of mobility come with costs. And the costs are all linked to the types of transportation that make mobility possible. Apart from walking and cycling, virtually all forms of transportation used today are dependent on oil as their energy source. However, oil is a non-renewable resource and, when burned (to release its energy), it sends harmful emissions into the Earth's atmosphere. This presents serious issues for both people and the environment.

FACT

More than 96 per cent of the world's transportation is dependent on oil.

VIEWPOINT

'Transportation is essential for moving people and goods, but it also has a broader role. It shapes our cities, stimulates economic growth and makes possible ...[social] interactions.'
Daniel Roos, Massachusetts Institute of Technology (MIT), USA

As car use increases so does traffic congestion, here shown in Shanghai, China.

Heating up

The biggest problem associated with transportation is the threat of climate change caused by the heating up of the Earth's atmosphere. This heating or 'global warming' is due to a build-up of certain gases in the atmosphere that act like a greenhouse, allowing the energy of the sun to reach the Earth and then trapping its heat. The most important greenhouse gas is carbon dioxide (CO_2) which is released when fossil fuels, such as oil, are burned. Although CO_2 is released from numerous sources, transportation is to blame for an increasingly large proportion of emissions. In 1999, it was estimated to account for around 26 per cent of CO_2 emissions from human activities.

A growing concern

Emissions of CO_2 from transportation are set to increase in future as the number of motor vehicles on the world's roads continues to grow. Already, in 2001, there were an estimated 700 million motor vehicles. With around 40 million new vehicles being produced each year, the number on the world's roads is expected to reach 1.1 billion by 2020. Air travel worldwide is also increasing rapidly and is expected to double between 1995 and 2015. This will add further to the CO_2 in the atmosphere, and increase the threat of climate change.

Warning signs

Many experts believe we are already seeing the first signs of climate change, with more frequent abnormal weather events such as droughts and floods. Glacier fields and the polar ice caps are also melting at an alarming rate due to an increase in average global temperatures. If such trends continue, whole regions of the world could be seriously threatened, not least by rising sea levels as the oceans warm and swell (water increases in volume as it gets warmer). Ironically, such changes could threaten the very mobility that is partly to blame for causing them. The challenge that lies ahead is to find ways of preserving mobility without harming the environment for future generations. This will demand a reassessment of transportation options for the twenty-first century. This book shares some of the ideas and opinions being expressed by the different contributors to this important debate.

FACT

Cars and trucks in the USA consume around 11 per cent of the world's annual oil production, but the USA accounts for just 5 per cent of world population.

DEBATE

Before reading on, think about your own use of transportation and how it affects others and the environment. See how many of those issues come up in the rest of the book.

Rescue workers tour the flooded historic streets of Meissen, near Dresden in Germany, after the River Elbe flooded in 2002. Experts believe that global warming, caused partly by emissions from transportation, could lead to similar scenes in many countries in the future.

REVOLUTIONS IN TRANSPORTATION

This donkey performs a vital role, carrying water in Kenya.

Continual change

The history of transportation is one of successive revolutions that have continually transformed the mobility of people and goods. These revolutions have shaped much of human history and determined the nature and location of human settlements and economies. Take the ancient Egyptians, for example. It was their ability to build feluccas (an Egyptian-style sailing boat), for use on the River Nile, that allowed them to transport the granite and other materials used to construct their magnificent temples.

In more recent times, there has been a revolutionary move away from walking – our natural form of motion – to modern forms of transportation such as the motor car or the aeroplane. And yet, despite incredible progress in transportation, people in many parts of the world continue to depend on forms of mobility that have changed little for thousands of years. In Kenya, for instance, donkeys are still widely used to move goods between farmers' fields and the markets. Similarly, camel trains still remain a vital form of transportation in desert regions such as those of North Africa.

A world of options?

In the early twenty-first century, it might seem that we live in a world full of transportation options. However, in reality, those options are not equally

In the hostile environment of the Egyptian desert, a camel is often a more reliable form of transportation than the modern car.

available to all. The availability and use of transportation is closely related to levels of economic development. One way to look at this relationship is to consider the number of cars per person in different regions or countries. In the wealthy nations of North America, Western Europe and Japan, for example, there is today one car for every two or three people. In poorer countries, such as India and China, there is only around one car for every 250 people. Similar inequalities in transportation can be seen in other sectors too, such as railways. For example, the UK has a railway network almost five times bigger than that of Nigeria, even though the UK is only about a quarter of Nigeria's area, and has a population that is less than half the size of Nigeria's.

VIEWPOINTS

'A community without roads does not have a way out.'
A poor man. Juncal, Ecuador, in World Bank, Voices of the Poor (2000)

'The relationship between transport and development is neither obvious nor simple. Simply building a road does not guarantee that development will take place.'
Department For International Development (DFID), UK, Transport Links website

VIEWPOINTS

Transportation and the economy

Improving transportation in poorer, less developed countries is essential to their economic development. In an increasingly competitive global economy, less developed countries need efficient and reliable transportation in order to attract foreign investment. This is nothing new. Throughout history, economies have been highly dependent on transportation for their success. The Industrial Revolution in nineteenth-century Britain, for example, was partly driven by improvements in transportation, firstly with the development of the canal network and later the railways. These allowed raw materials and finished goods to be moved around the country more easily. Factories were located close to these transport networks and workers soon followed in order to take advantage of the new job opportunities, turning towns into cities. As these industrial cities grew, so did the demand for transportation.

A train leaves Paddington Station, London, in 1892. At the time such transportation was considered revolutionary.

Overground, underground

With so many people in one location, it became cost-effective to run new forms of transport such as trams (or streetcars, as they are known in the

A tram or streetcar running on the streets of Toronto in Canada. Although dating back almost 150 years, trams are now making a comeback in many cities.

USA). The first horse-drawn trams began operating in London from 1860, but it was the invention of the dynamo (electrical generator) in 1869 that led to a sudden growth in tramways which could now be powered by electricity. By 1910, most cities in Europe and North America had developed tramway systems. They became the main form of urban transportation and, as the cities expanded into the suburbs, so did the tramways.

However, tramways could only use a fixed route because of the wires, tracks or cables needed to power them. The invention of the petrol engine solved this problem and provided more flexible transportation. By the 1940s, buses had replaced many tramways and the old tracks and cables were gradually removed. In some places, however, new fixed-route transportation systems took the place of tramways. Among the most important was the subway system (also known as the underground, metro or tube). The subway used space efficiently, by running trains in tunnels beneath the city instead of using up valuable surface land. London, Paris, New York, Boston and Budapest all had subway systems by 1905 and many other cities soon followed their lead, including Tokyo, Moscow and Chicago.

FACT

The first subway system in London was just 6 km long and used steam-powered trains. It opened in 1863 and carried 9.5 million people in its first year.

VIEWPOINT

VIEWPOINT

'In the 20th century, the automobile provided tremendous benefits, and raised the standard of living in much of the world. But it also had a major negative impact on the environment.'
Bill Ford, Chairman of the Board, Ford Motor Company

Personal transportation

Early transportation systems were developed to serve industry and, later, to transport workers from their homes to the factories and offices where they worked. As incomes increased and people began to enjoy more leisure time, a new demand for personal transportation began to emerge. The railways were one of the first ways in which people enjoyed transportation for personal reasons. In the UK, for example, people began to take to the trains in order to escape the overcrowding and pollution of the cities. By the 1930s, special day-trip services, such as the *Brighton Belle* and the *Bournemouth Belle*, were taking people from London to seaside resorts on the south coast.

Freedom of the road

The real revolution in personal transportation came with the development of the private motor car. Early models were expensive, but the development of mass production techniques led to cheaper cars, such as Ford's Model-T, which could be afforded by the masses. Ever since the introduction of the Model-T in 1908, private motoring has grown rapidly and is today the dominant form of transportation in the more developed regions of the world. The freedom that a private vehicle gave people has been the key to its success. Today, many people living in more developed countries consider this freedom to be a basic right, but for the vast majority living in less developed countries it remains beyond their reach.

Cars being manufactured in a factory in Detroit, USA, in around 1927. Mass production such as this dramatically reduced the costs of motor cars.

Onwards and upwards

As we move further into the twenty-first century, transportation and mobility is continuing to change. One of the most recent revolutions has taken place in the skies. Aircraft have become more efficient, leading to dramatic reductions in the cost of flying. Today, more people are flying than at any time in history. Short-haul flights have grown particularly fast and many are offered at budget prices, making flying an affordable transportation option even over short distances. One UK budget airline alone saw its annual passenger numbers increase from just 30,000 in 1995 to around 11.4 million in 2002. As more airlines offer cheap short-haul flights, it is likely that flying will play an increasingly important role in the ongoing revolutions in transportation.

Passengers board a Ryanair plane at Manchester Airport in the UK. Ryanair is one of Europe's largest low-cost airlines.

FACT

Between 1908 and 1927, Ford built over 15 million Model-Ts. Mass production techniques reduced the price of the Model-T from US$850 in 1908 to less than US$300 by 1925.

DEBATE

Progress in transportation has brought great benefits to the world, but how equally are those benefits shared by the entire world's population?

KING OF THE ROAD

A motorized world

It is a measure of its success that there are few places left in the world where the motor vehicle is not found. In its numerous shapes and forms, including cars, lorries and buses, the motor vehicle has become the world's most favoured method of transportation for both people and cargo. In fact it is so favoured that today's towns and cities are often planned around the needs of the motor vehicle rather than the needs of the people who live there. In Europe, for example, between 20 and 25 per cent of the land area of towns and cities is set aside as car parks and roads.

This motorway junction in California, USA, is part of an urban landscape increasingly dominated by roads and car parks.

The dominance of motor vehicles is spreading beyond urban areas too. Retail parks, industrial estates, leisure complexes and new housing developments are increasingly built in out-of-town locations. This 'urban sprawl', as it is often known, is both encouraged by, and encourages, the greater use of motor vehicles. As road networks expand to service urban sprawl, valuable farmland and scenic countryside are swallowed in their path. In any one location the change may seem small but, when examined at a regional, national, or even international scale, it becomes clear that we are creating an increasingly motorized world.

Good for the economy?

Politicians often support the growth of motor vehicle networks because they believe they are good for the economy and will generate more trade and employment. There is little doubt that many towns, regions and indeed whole countries have benefited from improvements in such networks. In East Africa, for example, many of the more prosperous settlements are located along the Trans-African Highway which passes directly through the region. Just a few kilometres away from the highway, levels of poverty are much higher.

The increased wealth brought by road networks leads in turn to higher levels of vehicle ownership, as incomes increase. In time, this results in road networks becoming congested with too much traffic. This can harm the economy, as time and money is wasted in traffic jams and delays. In the UK, for example, the annual cost to the economy of traffic congestion is estimated to be at least US$16 billion. Meanwhile, in the USA up to two billion hours are wasted each year by urban residents sitting in traffic jams.

VIEWPOINTS

'We believe that everyone involved in transportation policy should recognize that personal mobility is an essential tool for promoting economic growth and a vital component of today's busy lifestyles.'
Ford Motor Company website

'We should ... do away with the simplistic notion that "more cars" equals "more economic growth".'
Federico Mayor and Jérôme Bindé. The World Ahead, 2001

An unhealthy habit

Our increasing dependence on motor vehicles is an issue of growing concern for human health. Nearly all motor vehicles run on petroleum-based fuels, such as petrol and diesel. As these fuels are burned, a variety of waste gases and particles are released, some of which are harmful to human health. In urban areas, where traffic levels are at their highest, the problems are particularly severe, especially for those who suffer from breathing disorders such as asthma or bronchitis.

Emissions from motor vehicles contribute to this mid-afternoon smog in Beijing, China.

Among the most dangerous motor-related pollutants is lead, which is added to petrol to improve vehicle performance. When released into the atmosphere, even in relatively small quantities, it can cause lead poisoning in humans. The effects of lead poisoning can include headaches, stomach pains, tremors and in severe cases even death. Lead is especially harmful to young children as it affects the development of the brain. Since the 1970s, lead has gradually been removed from fuels in North America and Europe but it is still used in many less developed countries. In Cairo, Egypt, for example, levels of atmospheric lead in the more congested districts are up to six times higher than those considered safe by the World Health Organization (WHO). Across Africa as a whole, up to 90 per cent of children living in major urban centres are thought to suffer the effects of lead poisoning.

Cleaning the air

In an effort to reduce air pollution from motor vehicles, governments now have numerous regulations to limit emissions and clean up the air. For example, motor vehicles in the UK and USA must today pass increasingly strict emissions tests in order to be allowed on the road. In the UK, poor vehicle maintenance and inaccurate testing is said to mean that 10 to 20 per cent of vehicles on the nation's roads fail to meet emissions targets. However, cleaner fuels, such as low sulphur petrol and diesel, are helping the situation. These fuels have lessened sulphur emissions by around two-thirds from petrol vehicles and 90 per cent from diesel vehicles. By 2000, all diesel vehicles in the UK were using ultra low sulphur diesel.

> ## VIEWPOINT
>
> '...clearly, global warming is a real issue. And even if you don't believe in climate change, there are other problems. Travel to places like Beijing and Mexico City and you can almost cut the air with a knife.'
> *Bill Ford, Chairman of the Board, Ford Motor Company*

Many authorities have introduced random vehicle emissions testing to try to limit air pollution caused by motor vehicles. This roadside testing station is in London, UK.

FACT

In Bangkok, Thailand, 524 cars were being added to the city's roads every day in 1990. By 2000, this had fallen a little but was still an incredible 481 per day!

Acid rain has destroyed these trees near Litvinov, in the Czech Republic.

Road to ruin

The impact of vehicle emissions on human health has lessened dramatically since the 1980s. But some of the most significant waste gases, including nitrogen oxides (NOx), sulphur dioxide (SO_2) and carbon dioxide (CO_2), continue to be released in substantial quantities. NOx and SO_2 are major causes of acid rain, while CO_2 is the main gas responsible for the warming of the atmosphere and predicted changes in world climate. In 1999, road transportation accounted for 16.9 per cent of total CO_2 emissions, the same as from all forms of transportation in 1971.

The proportion of global CO_2 emissions from motor vehicles is set to increase further as the number of vehicles on the world's roads continues to grow. Much of this future increase will come from less developed countries where car use is growing most rapidly. In South Korea, for example, the number of motor vehicles on the nation's roads increased by an incredible 1,710 per cent between 1980 and 1996. This massive growth led to an increase in motor vehicle CO_2 emissions of 2,183 per cent over the same period.

Even where the number of vehicles is growing more slowly, CO_2 emissions are growing disproportionately because people are travelling further than at any time in the past. In the USA, for instance, the annual distance driven by passenger cars increased four-fold between 1950 and 1999. In the UK, there was a fifteen-fold increase over the same period. Such worrying patterns have led many people to believe that motor vehicles are driving us along a road to environmental ruin.

Technology to the rescue?

Those in the motor industry point out that technological improvements over the last few decades have made vehicles more efficient and less polluting. A vehicle made today, for example, produces less than 5 per cent of the emissions of its 1960s equivalent. However, while welcoming such changes, critics argue that there is room for further improvement. For instance, a European Union (EU) study found that the technology already exists to reduce fuel consumption in an average petrol car by around 40 per cent. A similar study by the Sierra Club, a major US environmental organization, found that a typical family car could be made 54 per cent more fuel-efficient by using the latest technology.

VIEWPOINT

'Advances in transportation technology have brought benefits, but growing vehicle fleets and escalating fuel use have also created problems.'
Molly O'Meara Sheehan, Worldwatch Institute, USA

weblinks

For more information on improved fuel efficiency of cars, go to www.waylinks.co.uk/series/21debates/transportation

VIEWPOINT

'The automobile industry's record for introducing environmental technology over the last few decades is really poor. We need the government to step in and force the automakers to build more fuel-efficient vehicles.'
Jason Mark, director of the Union of Concerned Scientists (UCS) Clean Vehicles Program

A sustainable future?

Harvesting sugar cane in Cuba. Sugar cane can be used to make a form of bio-fuel for vehicles.

The bad news is that motor vehicle numbers and use are set to continue growing. But there is also some good news, in the form of new sustainable fuel technologies. These include biodiesel which is made from vegetable oils and can be used in a pure form or as a blend with oil-based diesel. As a cleaner alternative to diesel, biodiesel produces fewer emissions and is renewable because it is based on plant extracts. In the USA, biodiesel was being used by over a hundred major vehicle fleets in 2002, including those of the US postal service, the US Army, the US Department of Energy, and the National Aeronautics and Space Administration (NASA).

The most exciting prospect for future motoring is the development of the hydrogen fuel cell. This combines hydrogen with oxygen to create electrical energy that can be used to power a vehicle. The only waste product is water vapour and so hydrogen fuel cells have the potential to be a completely sustainable and emission-free technology. Several motor manufacturers are developing fuel cell powered vehicles and the technology is already being used in trial buses in North America and Europe. The problem, say critics, is that hydrogen fuel is currently extracted from existing fossil fuels (which are made up of hydrogen and carbon) and so is not sustainable. It is possible to produce hydrogen from water, however, by splitting it into hydrogen and oxygen, using a process called electrolysis. Electrolysis itself uses a lot of energy, but if this came from renewable sources (such as wind or solar power) then hydrogen fuel cells could be used to power zero-emission motor vehicles.

VIEWPOINT

'America can lead the world in developing clean, hydrogen-powered automobiles. With a new national commitment, our scientists and engineers will overcome obstacles to taking these cars from laboratory to showroom.'
President George W. Bush, State of the Union Address, 2003

This bus is one of a new generation of zero-emission buses now on trial around the world. They use hydrogen fuel cells as their power source, a technology that has the potential to bring clean motoring to future generations.

New attitudes

No matter how clean new technology is, issues such as congestion and traffic accidents will continue to make motor vehicles a problematic means of transportation. The solution, many now believe, lies in changing people's attitudes to transportation and encouraging them to use a variety of different options instead. This is easier said than done, however, as many people have become very attached to their motor vehicles and the freedom of mobility that they believe they offer. The next four chapters look at some of the alternatives to motor vehicles and consider both their positive and negative contributions to the transportation debate.

weblinks

For more information
on fuel cells, go to
www.waylinks.co.uk/series/
21debates/transportation

DEBATE

Does technological progress, such as the development of improved, cleaner fuels, mean that we can ignore the problems caused by motor vehicle use?

TAKING TO THE AIR

Up, up and away!

As we move further into the twenty-first century, one of the fastest-growing transportation sectors is air travel. Advances in technology mean that aircraft are today much bigger and able to carry far more passengers than in the past. The largest can now accommodate up to 550 passengers. They have also become more fuel-efficient, due to better engine design, and the use of lightweight construction materials and improved aviation fuels. Passenger jets produced in 2002, for example, used around three times less fuel per seat-kilometre than jets built in the 1960s. This remarkable efficiency improvement, of around 66 per cent, compares with gains of between 15 and 30 per cent for road and rail transportation.

A 747 passenger jet, one of several long-range aircraft that have transformed international air travel.

As a result of all these technological improvements, jets can today fly further than at any time in the past. For instance, the latest Boeing 747-400 (popularly known as 'Jumbo') passenger jets have a range of an incredible 14,205 km. This enables them to fly non-stop from New York to Hong Kong or from London to Singapore.

Even more dramatic than the improvements in aviation technology over the last fifty years has been the

growth in actual air travel. By 2000, the total number of passengers using air transportation for business and tourism had reached around 1.6 billion. And this is expected to increase further to an amazing 2.3 billion passengers a year by 2010. The majority of these passengers are from the more developed regions of the world where air travel is more established. For instance, Europe accounts for around 58 per cent of all air passengers, while the USA has one of the most established air transportation networks. Its commercial air fleet made over 8.8 million scheduled departures in 2001.

Global air transportation of cargo is growing even faster than that of passengers, at around 11 per cent a year since 1960. In 2001, around 29 million tonnes of freight cargo (which represented 40 per cent of the world's manufactured exports by value) was transported by air.

VIEWPOINT

'Where flying was once a privilege, even for the affluent, it's now a given in the lives of the vast majority of UK citizens.'
Jonathan Porritt, programme director, Forum for the Future, UK

FACT

In 2000, Hartsfield International Airport, Atlanta, USA, was the busiest in the world, handling 915,657 flights and 80.2 million passengers.

Air freight sits on the tarmac in Hong Kong before its onward journey. Air freight is a fast-growing transportation sector.

FACT

Of the 1,190 islands in the Maldives, only 200 are inhabited. Eighty-seven of them are exclusive resort islands.

New opportunities

In an era in which business and trade is increasingly conducted at a global level, air transportation has brought new opportunities to many less developed countries and areas that were previously remote and cut-off. Kenya, in East Africa, is a good example. Farmers there have been able to take advantage of improvements in air freight to export fresh fruit, vegetables and flowers (collectively known as horticultural goods) to lucrative markets in Europe and the Middle East. By 2001, the horticulture industry accounted for 44 per cent of Kenya's exports to the European Union and was the country's third most important source of foreign exchange (after tourism and tea). This is particularly extraordinary given the fact that in 1990 the horticulture industry hardly existed in Kenya. New handling facilities at Nairobi Airport and the opening of a new airport in Eldoret in 1998 have ensured that the industry continues to grow and take advantage of air freight developments.

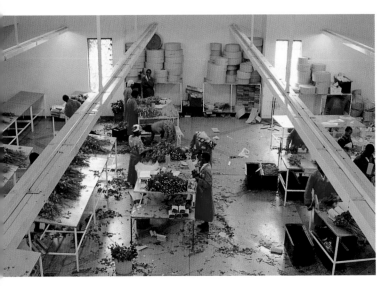

Flowers being packed at lunchtime in Kenya will be in European supermarkets the following day, thanks to advances in air freight.

Tourism has been one of the main industries to benefit from air transportation, accounting for almost 60 per cent of international air passengers by 2000. The majority of international tourists travel by plane, and runways and airports have been constructed in order to make many new destinations more accessible. For example, the Maldives, a remote chain of 1,190 islands in the Indian Ocean, have become a popular tourist destination following the construction of Hulule International Airport.

From there, tourists are transferred by boat-planes or speedboats and ferries to other islands in the chain. The airport has enabled tourism to grow into the most important industry in the Maldives, accounting for around 60 per cent of the island's foreign exchange earnings.

Hulule International Airport, in the Maldives, shows that few places are beyond the reach of modern transportation. Located in the middle of the Indian Ocean, this amazing airstrip looks more like an aircraft carrier than an island.

A mixed blessing

The increased access that air transportation allows can also bring problems however. As tourist numbers grow, so too does the demand for accommodation, food, water, wood-fuel and other goods and services. Supplying these can cause resentment among local people, as resources become scarcer. Pressure from tourists can also damage local environments. For instance, in Nepal, a destination that most visitors access by air, serious environmental problems of deforestation, erosion and litter have been caused by an increase in the number of trekkers visiting the country.

FACT

In 1998, 43 per cent of international tourists travelled by air. In less developed countries, over 90 per cent of international tourists arrived by air.

VIEWPOINTS

'The costs of failing to expand [airport] capacity for the travelling public will be felt through more delays, less choice in routes and connecting traffic, higher fares and fewer regional air links.'
Brenda Dean, Chair, Freedom to Fly, UK

'People who live close to airports suffer more than mere annoyance from ascending and descending aircraft. Beyond annoyance, aircraft noise may have significant mental and physical health impacts on people who live below the flight path of commercial and private airplanes.'
League for the Hard of Hearing, New York, USA

FACT

Air tickets would cost 20 to 30 per cent more for short-haul flights and 5 per cent more for long-haul flights if the environmental costs of emissions and noise were included in the price.

High-level polluters

Air transportation currently produces around 2 per cent of global CO_2 emissions from human sources. However, if air traffic continues to increase as expected, emission levels are set to treble by 2050. Emissions from aircraft are particularly damaging because they are released at high altitude where they are known to do more damage than those released at ground level. The airline industry is constantly improving the efficiency of aircraft (and therefore reducing emissions) as fuel is one of its major costs, but the growing number of aircraft in use means the total volume of emissions continues to grow. Long-haul flights are less polluting than short-haul flights, because take-offs are the most polluting stage of the journey. However, with falling air fares, short-haul flights have become one of the fastest-growing sectors, especially in Europe.

To meet the increasing demand for short-haul flights, many local and regional airports are being extended and new ones are being opened. Such developments, while perhaps benefiting the local economy, often irritate local residents who fear an increase in local air pollution and high levels of noise pollution. Although airports are inevitably noisy places, careful planning of their location and improved aircraft design can all help to reduce the problem. Aircraft used today are around 75 per cent quieter than those made in 1970. This means that fewer people are disturbed by noise, despite the increase in air traffic.

For the good of people

Besides economic benefits, air transportation has brought significant humanitarian gains too. For example, in Australia the 'flying doctor' service provides medical care for remote communities living beyond the drivable range of a hospital or clinic. In 2000, the service's forty-five aircraft flew

TAKING TO THE AIR

more than 4.5 million km, and visited some 185,000 patients. Aircraft are also used for humanitarian aid missions, such as getting food or medical supplies to areas struck by natural disasters. Air transportation enables emergency services to respond much more rapidly than they could using land- or water-based forms of transportation. And, in doing so, it saves thousands of lives every year.

Aircraft allow the 'flying doctor' service in Australia to reach even the most remote communities and deliver vital healthcare services to thousands of people.

Year	Percentage increase in global passenger km flown since 1990
2000	36
2015	115*
2030	239*
2050	524*

Source: Air Transport Action Group (ATAG) and United Nations Environment Programme (UNEP), 2002

* Predicted increases

DEBATE

Should we be building more airports to encourage the continued rapid growth of air transportation?

GETTING BACK ON TRACK

Swedish trains are well-used by passengers and well-maintained, despite a decline in the Swedish rail network over recent years.

Changing fortunes

The railway was once the backbone of most national transportation systems. It supported the development of early industries and offered many people their first experience of affordable travel. However, since the 1930s, road transportation (for both commercial and leisure purposes) has increasingly replaced the railway as the most favoured form of transport. One of the main reasons for the decline of the railways was that they could not offer the 'door to door' service provided by motorized transport. As a result, many railway networks have declined. The French rail network, for example, reduced its track length by around 9 per cent between 1980 and 1999, while Swedish railways showed a 12 per cent reduction over the same period.

Despite declining networks, the number of rail passengers has actually been increasing in many countries. For example, in Sweden, rail passengers increased by almost 50 per cent between 1980 and 1999. And in the UK, rail passengers increased by 17 per cent over the same period, even though the network continued to shrink.

Many networks have declined due to low usage, making certain routes unprofitable. But others, especially in less developed countries, have declined due to an overall lack of maintenance and investment. In East Africa, for instance, the once important East African Railway, which runs through Uganda and Kenya, is now barely passable in some places; derailments, delays and cancellations have become very common. Today the East African Railway is mainly used for freight transport, but there are ambitious plans to revive it for both cargo and passenger traffic in the future.

A railway yard in Nairobi, Kenya, showing out-of-service passenger cars in the sidings. Freight trains are still in operation however.

Bearing the load

There has also been less movement of freight or cargo on the railways, as road haulage has become more widely used. In the UK, for instance, railway freight fell from 157.2 million tonnes in 1980 to 107.2 million tonnes in 1999. Japan, France and Germany, among other countries, also experienced a decline in rail freight. By contrast, rail freight has increased in North America and many less developed countries. In India, for example, the amount of freight carried by rail more than doubled between 1980 and 1999 to 463.3 million tonnes.

FACT

In 2000, 1.6 billion tonnes of freight was moved by rail in the USA – more than any other country except China (which transported almost 1.8 billion tonnes).

VIEWPOINT

'More freight on rail is a worthwhile objective. It is good for Great Britain ... for our environment and for the transport system on which our individual way of life depends.'
Chairman. UK Strategic Rail Authority (SRA). 2001

FACT

Railroads in the USA move more than four times as much freight as do all of Western Europe's freight railroads combined.

— **weblinks** —

For more information on rail freight or roadrailer technology, go to www.waylinks.co.uk/series/ 21debates/transportation

Vital link

Rail networks remain vital for many industries that need to move large quantities of bulky or heavy items. In the mining industry, for instance, railways are frequently used to transport raw materials to processing plants or to ports for export. In Jamaica, the only railway still running today is a privately owned line used to transport bauxite (needed to make aluminium) from the island's bauxite mines. And in the UK, the railway remains the main mode of transport used to deliver coal to the country's coal-fired power stations which provided around 33.5 per cent of UK electricity in 2001.

As roads become more congested in the future, many rail networks expect to see an increase in demand for freight transportation. In the UK, for example, the government hopes to increase rail freight by 80 per cent between 2000 and 2010. If achieved, this increase would be a significant factor in easing congestion on the roads. (An average freight train can replace the equivalent of fifty heavy goods vehicles on the road network.) In addition, rail freight produces around 80 per cent fewer CO_2 emissions than road transport for each tonne that is carried, and has been shown to be twenty-seven times safer than transporting goods by road.

This Australian freight train can carry heavy goods across vast distances cheaply, safely and efficiently.

Greater flexibility

Many companies are unwilling to use rail freight because they believe it to be inflexible. Freight companies argue, however, that improved links with road transportation will help develop a 21st-century door-to-door service for rail freight. A central part of this is the development of containerization. This involves the use of standard-sized containers for the transportation of freight, thus allowing easy transfer between different transport modes such as ships, trains, aircraft and lorries.

VIEWPOINT

'We move over 2 billion tonnes of goods around the UK each year, an amount which is set to grow. But people don't want heavier lorries. They want more investment in, and incentives for rail.'
Tara Garnett. Freight on Rail campaigner. UK

In the USA, this type of intermodal freight transportation involving the railway almost trebled between 1980 and 2000, with 69 per cent of freight being transported in containers. New technological developments, such as roadrailers, are likely to increase intermodal use of the railways even further. Roadrailers look like normal lorry trailers, but can ride directly on railway tracks by using an extra set of steel rail wheels and raising the road wheels off the ground during rail transit.

These containers, waiting to be unloaded from ships at a container port in Hamburg, Germany, can be easily transferred to road or rail modes of transportation.

Rail for leisure

Some railway lines that have fallen out of commercial passenger or freight use are today finding new life as leisure attractions. In the USA, for example, the Grand Canyon Railway, which was first established in 1901 to serve local mines, is now a popular tourist line. Today it takes almost 170,000 visitors a year from the town of Williams to the rim of the Grand Canyon – one of the world's greatest natural wonders. In California, the Napa Valley Wine Train is equally popular as an alternative way to view the region's famous vineyards. Elsewhere in the world, trains such as the luxurious Orient Express in Europe and South Africa's Blue Train preserve memories of a bygone era when rail provided the most elegant, stylish way to travel.

weblinks

For more information on tourist trains, go to www.waylinks.co.uk/series/21debates/transportation

A steam engine on the Grand Canyon Railway in Arizona, USA, once used for the mining industry, is today preserved as a tourist attraction.

New direction

These days, the fastest-growing forms of rail transportation are light rail systems, which are increasingly being used for short-distance travel in urban centres across the world. Light rail uses tracks that are either sunken into existing roads and streets or run on elevated sections above street level. Being cheaper to install than alternatives such as metro systems, light rail is a popular option for relieving traffic congestion in relatively small cities. In the UK, for example, Sheffield (with a population of 513,000 in 2001) and Nottingham (with a population of 267,000) both have light rail systems in operation. In the USA, twenty-five cities had light rail systems by 2000, with many more planned for the future.

This light rail system in central Sydney, Australia, provides a quick and convenient method of transportation and an interesting view of the city below!

Supporters of light rail systems point out that they are highly effective at reducing car journeys and regenerating urban centres. In the USA, for instance, St Louis' light rail link carried around 42,000 passengers every weekday in 2001, 80 per cent of whom used to travel by car. Meanwhile, the Metropolitan Area Express (MAX) light rail in Portland, USA, has helped regenerate the city centre and avoided the need to build eight multi-storey car parks and widen roads linking the city to the suburbs. Critics of light rail believe that it simply creates road space that is quickly filled by more motorists. But, despite these concerns, there is little doubt that light rail continues to improve mobility for thousands of urban and suburban residents across the world.

DEBATE

Should more city centre roads be converted to run light rail systems? What reasons would you give to support your argument?

WATERWAYS

Liquid asset

Water has a long history as an important means of transportation and many of the world's greatest settlements – including New York, London, Cape Town, Rio de Janeiro, Shanghai and Tokyo – are located on waterways or by the coast. They have developed there because of the economic benefits offered by water-borne transportation and, despite the success of railways, motor vehicles and aircraft, this form of transportation remains very important today.

There are several reasons for this. Firstly, no other form of transport is able to match the carrying capacity of cargo vessels; and rivers and canals continue to perform a vital role in connecting inland areas with the coast. The Mississippi river in the USA, for example, transports around 472 million tonnes of cargo a year, including almost half the USA's grain exports. Although transportation by water is much slower than other forms, this is more than made up for by the amount that can be carried. In the USA, for instance, a standard tow barge with fifteen barges can transport the equivalent of 870 road haulage trucks. If travelling in a convoy, spaced 46 m (150 feet) apart, that number of trucks would stretch for 56 km (35 miles)!

Secondly, there is the question of cost. Studies in the UK, published in 2002, showed that transporting freight by river was up to five times cheaper than transporting it by road. Supporters of inland water transportation claim that more businesses could take advantage of waterways if they simply planned their freight movements further in advance. In a world that is moving at an ever-faster pace, however, many businesses see inland waterways as a rather outdated mode of transport.

Oceans apart

International water transportation, across the world's oceans, is an essential part of the modern global economy. Raw materials and finished goods are carried vast distances across the globe in this way. Foods, too, including some of the tropical vegetables and fruits now regularly made available to shoppers in colder climates such as Europe and North America, are increasingly shipped over vast distances. Vast ports such as Rotterdam, in the Netherlands, and Shanghai, in China, have developed on the basis of this trade. Rotterdam alone handled 322 million tonnes of freight in 2002.

The yachts moored here at Causeway Bay in Hong Kong show that links between road and ocean transportation are important for leisure as well as for trade and industry.

FACT

The largest cargo vessel in the world is the *Jahre Viking* oil tanker. It is 458.45 metres long and weighs an incredible 564,763 tonnes – the equivalent of around 374,000 typical family cars!

weblinks

To find out about the world's busiest port, go to www.waylinks.co.uk/series/21debates/transportation

VIEWPOINT

'There are hundreds of older vessels in the world fleet that are simply ticking time bombs. The fact is they shouldn't be allowed to carry toxic cargoes, never mind pass anywhere near pristine coastlines.'

Anonymous European salvage expert, Planet Ark news service

Passenger traffic

Besides freight, water transportation is also used to carry people for business, leisure and tourism purposes. For example, in the Swedish capital, Stockholm, a city divided by numerous rivers and channels, passenger ferries are a regular part of the city's public transport system. For longer-distance travel – for instance between the UK and Europe across the English Channel – larger ferries (which also carry vehicles) are one of the most common forms of transportation. Dover, the UK's busiest port, was used by some 16 million passengers and 2.5 million cars and buses in 2002. Longer journeys, such as transatlantic crossings, are today mainly taken by tourists as part of the rapidly growing cruise industry. And within countries such as France, the UK and the Netherlands, many people enjoy taking leisurely boating holidays and excursions on rivers and canals.

River boats wait for their passengers on the River Volga in Russia.

Disrupting nature

However there are some downsides to water transportation. Firstly, in order for it to operate efficiently, considerable changes often have to be made to the surrounding environment. Rivers are straightened, dredged, redirected or dammed, for example, while coastal environments are cleared to make way for big ports. The adaptation of rivers to encourage transportation can be particularly disruptive to natural environments and processes. It can change the flow of water and in times of high flow lead to devastating flooding as the river tries to regain its natural course. The Yangtze, in China, regularly suffers from such flooding. And in the USA, the Mississippi river burst through several levees (artificial embankments) in 1993, causing US$12 billion worth of damage and halting river transportation for two months.

Other environmental impacts include the sometimes serious damage water craft can do to aquatic species through accidents and pollution. For example, in India, numbers of the now endangered Ganges river dolphin have fallen dramatically because of accidents with boat propellers and pollution from boat engines. Spills from the vast oil tankers that transport fuel around the world are perhaps the biggest environmental hazard of water transportation. For instance, when the *Exxon Valdez* ran aground off Alaska in 1989 it spilled 257,000 barrels of oil along 320 km (200 miles) of Alaskan coastline, causing the deaths of an estimated 350,000 seabirds.

Improving rivers for transportation often requires protective measures such as levees (earth embankments). This aerial view of the Atchafalaya river, in Louisiana, USA, shows the high levees that have been built along the river basin.

Responsible shipping

Following accidents such as the *Exxon Valdez*, and many that have happened since, new international standards have been agreed to phase out the older and more hazardous ships currently using the world's waterways. By 2015, all oil tankers will have to be double-hulled instead of single-hulled ships such as the *Exxon Valdez*. This will ensure that their cargo is better protected and will make spillage less likely if they hit submerged objects or are involved in a collision. However it may prove difficult to enforce such regulations, and some single-hulled vessels will probably continue to operate illegally beyond the 2015 deadline.

One of the biggest problems in enforcing shipping regulations is the fact that it is such an international industry. Take the example of the oil tanker *Prestige* which sank off Spain in November 2002, releasing 10,000 tonnes of oil and taking a further 65,000 tonnes with it to the bottom of the ocean. At the time, the *Prestige* was carrying oil from Latvia to Singapore for a Russian trading company based in Switzerland. The ship itself was Liberian-owned, but registered in the Bahamas. When it sank, it was operated by a Greek-based company and had been passed as seaworthy by an American shipping authority. With so many different groups involved, it can be difficult to decide who should take responsibility when things go wrong and who should be responsible for putting them right!

Following the *Prestige* sinking, many environmentalists and politicians have called for the ban on single-hulled vessels to be brought forward. According to some reports, the ban could be achieved by 2010-2012, but many shipping companies say that bringing the deadline forward is simply not possible. They say that time is needed

Volunteers clean up the oil spilled by the tanker Prestige *on the Spanish coast in November 2002. Such incidents are a dramatic reminder of the risks involved in transporting hazardous cargoes by ocean.*

for the massive investment and construction process needed to build new double-hulled oil tankers. There are fewer shipyards able to build such vessels than in the past and there are concerns that rushing in the new regulations could lead to poor-quality vessels. This could raise the chances of a disaster even further in the future.

DEBATE

Given the risks involved in transporting oil by water, is our dependence on oil as the main transport-ation fuel still a sensible transportation option in the twenty-first century?

RECLAIMING THE STREETS

Back to basics

In many towns and cities across the world, communities are deciding that they have had enough of the problems brought about by existing transportation options. They have a right to be concerned, for the problems are many – including city air thick with pollution, buses delayed by traffic jams, roads too dangerous to cycle on, and priority given to cars instead of pedestrians. But now there is a growing call to rethink urban transportation and, in many cases, go back to basics, by encouraging a revival of non-motorized modes of transport such as walking and cycling.

Nothing new

Of course there is nothing new about walking or cycling. Walking is humankind's most ancient and natural method of moving from one place to another, and is still the dominant form of mobility for much of the world's population. In less developed countries (where the vast majority of the world's population lives), people often have little choice but to walk. In villages throughout sub-Saharan Africa, for example, it is common for people to walk for several hours a day just to perform basic tasks such as collecting water or fuel wood. In addition to the time and distance involved, this places an enormous physical burden on those who regularly carry loads of 20 kg or more. In such circumstances, alternatives to walking are required in order to make people's day-to-day lives easier and to help the development of local economies.

With little alternative, these Kenyan women regularly carry heavy loads on their heads.

In Europe and North America, the bicycle is often considered a rather old-fashioned and basic form of transportation, reserved today for recreation and leisure rides. In the USA, for example, the number of young people aged between seven and seventeen who rode a bicycle more than once a year fell by 13 per cent between 1990 and 1999. In stark contrast, bicycles are seen as prized possessions in many less developed countries. They greatly improve mobility for the poor, allowing easier access to markets and reducing the burden of carrying heavy loads on foot. Bicycles can also help in the provision of essential services such as health and education. In Ghana, West Africa, bicycles given to HIV/AIDS educators have helped them communicate their vital message to 50 per cent more people than have been reached by those educators working on foot.

VIEWPOINT

'...cycling is still often linked in the public mind to a society that pre-dates affluence and prosperity. The use of bicycles must be transformed into a point of pride, with the emphasis on its advantages as a silent, flexible, non-polluting means of transport, excellent for health and requiring little infrastructure.'
Federico Mayor and Jérôme Bindé, The World Ahead, 2001

Encouraging signs

Recent trends suggest that bicycle use is increasing. In 2000, for example, 101 million bicycles were produced worldwide (more than twice the number of motor vehicles and the highest production figures since 1995). At the same time, the infrastructure needed to encourage greater cycling is receiving a welcome boost in many countries. In the UK, for instance, an extensive network of cycle paths and cycle-safe routes was opened in 2000 as part of the National Cycle Network. In 2002, an estimated 97.2 million trips were made on the 10,860 km (6,750 mile) network, a figure set to grow as the network extends to 16,000 km (10,000 miles) by 2005.

Practical solutions

One of the biggest barriers to cycling is that it is not always a practical transportation solution. Those living in hilly areas, for example, may find it too difficult to cycle regularly, while some elderly people may find even cycling on the level too much of a strain. New developments, such as electric bicycles (e-bicycles), can help solve such

VIEWPOINTS

'Cities can actively promote walking and cycling by investing in bike paths and racks, slowing cars, and making streets physically appealing. Studies of cycling investments in Amsterdam [the Netherlands], Bogotá [Colombia], Morogoro [Tanzania], and Delhi [India], found that small investments can yield great benefits.'
Molly O'Meara Sheehan.
Research Associate.
Worldwatch Institute. USA

'Bikes may be fun on a sunny afternoon, but who wants to cycle in winter rain? Problems of weather-protection, security and baggage capacity, all put cycling at a severe disadvantage, despite its environmental benefits.'
Richard Buckley.
Understanding Global Issues:
Avoiding Gridlock. 1997

weblinks

For more information on the UK National Cycle Network, go to www.waylinks.co.uk/series/ 21debates/transportation

Policemen use bicycles on duty at Venice Beach, California, USA.

problems. In 2000, the world sales of e-bicycles reached 1.1 million – three times the number sold in 1999. E-bicycles are especially popular in China where they are regularly used by commuters. They are also gaining in popularity in the USA where several police forces now use them – in cities like Chicago and Dallas. Officers on bicycles have been shown to reach crime scenes quicker than those struggling through traffic in squad cars – and typically make 50 per cent more arrests.

FACT

China, India and Taiwan produced 65 million bicycles in 1999, over half of which were exported.

In central Copenhagen, Denmark, free bikes are provided, to be used by members of the public.

If cycling is to be further encouraged, facilities such as secure parking for bicycles and cycle lock-ups at stations, colleges and places of work will also need improving. Where this has been done in combination with developing cycle routes it has led to high rates of cycle use. In Copenhagen, Denmark, for example, some 30 per cent of commuters travel to work by bicycle, while in the Netherlands up to half of city journeys are made by bicycle. Even in the USA, where cycling is on the decline, an estimated 3 million people get to work each day by bicycle.

FACT

An e-bicycle can usually travel at speeds of up to 29 km (18 miles) per hour, unassisted by pedalling.

weblinks

For more information about 'home zones', go to www.waylinks.co.uk/series/21debates/transportation

It makes sense

Making walking and cycling easier and more appealing not only helps to improve the quality of urban environments and people's health, it can also make good economic sense. Cycling, in particular, is often the quickest and most efficient way to move around congested urban streets. In London, for example, a government survey in 1996 found that a 2.7 km (1.7 mile) journey took cyclists an average of just 18 minutes to complete, compared to 33 minutes for those travelling by car and 38 minutes by bus.

A bicycle courier cycles down Fifth Avenue in New York, USA. Bicycles can be the fastest way to move goods around increasingly congested city streets in many parts of the world.

RECLAIMING THE STREETS

Courier firms are increasingly taking advantage of the greater mobility bicycles allow, and sending out bicycle messengers to negotiate busy city streets. In New York, some 300 bicycle messenger firms compete for US$700 million worth of business per year. In Sydney, however, bicycle couriers have been criticized for endangering others' safety by riding on pavements, jumping traffic lights and ignoring one-way streets. Complaints led the city council to introduce new regulations for bicycle couriers from 2003.

Home zones

Although pedestrianized city centres may be a familiar sight today, it is less common to see whole streets that have been made more people-friendly. This is beginning to change, however, with the spread of 'home zones'. Home zones involve traffic-calming measures (such as speed bumps), speed limits of 16-32 km (10-20 miles) per hour, and changes of priority so that motorists must give way to pedestrians and cyclists. In addition, home zones are often planted with trees and flower beds and may have benches, play areas or works of street art. In the Netherlands, home zones have proven extremely popular, with over 6,500 now in place across the country. Germany, Austria and Denmark have also adopted the home zones idea and it is currently being trialled in the UK and USA.

Despite the benefits they offer, home zones in the UK and USA have met with some resistance. In the UK, there have been complaints about traffic tailbacks and slower response times for emergency vehicles. Meanwhile, in the USA, residents have asked for traffic restrictions to be removed because they can no longer park their cars outside their homes. So it seems that home zones may only become widespread if they are part of bigger changes in transportation policy.

VIEWPOINTS

'Historically streets were places where people lived, met, played, traded and travelled. They were busy places: the heart of the community. But today streets are congested with traffic rather than busy people. They are seen as a source of danger.'
Transport 2000 Trust, UK

'Home zones are streets where you can enjoy taking time to stop and chat with your neighbours. Streets where cars are allowed, but the car driver is a guest. They are common and popular in many European countries.'
Home Zone News, Children's Play Council, UK

DEBATE

Would you like to see your local street made into a home zone? What would the benefits and drawbacks be for your street?

TRANSPORTATION PLANNING

Thinking ahead!

It may seem obvious to say that transportation requires careful planning, but it is sometimes surprising how little thought goes into new projects and policies. Traffic lights, for example, are rarely timed for the benefit of pedestrians, even though it is those on foot who have to stand in the cold and rain waiting to cross while motorists whizz past in their warm, dry vehicles.

Government transport policies often seem to be very short-sighted. For instance, the continued emphasis on creating more road capacity in many countries ignores the fact that motorized transport is causing great harm to environments and human health. Motorized transport is also, at present, dependent on oil – a non-renewable resource. Instead, argue environmentalists and an increasing number of urban planners, we should be looking for transportation solutions that reduce our

An enormous area of land is cleared to make way for yet another new motorway being built in the UK.

dependence on the car. The challenge is to find a way of doing this without damaging the economy or reducing personal freedom or mobility.

Working together

The key to transportation planning is to achieve greater coordination between the different modes (transport methods) available.

Waiting times can discourage many people from using forms of public transport.

Containerization in the freight industry is a good example of this, and has significantly speeded up the movement of freight between different transport modes. However, moving people in a coordinated fashion can be much more complex than moving goods. Different modes of transport follow different timetables and run on set routes so getting from A to B can prove complicated and frustrating. For instance, delays to an inter-city rail service may cause passengers to miss a local rail connection and so extend their journey time significantly.

The same problem often occurs at a more local level with difficulties in synchronizing bus services or in sychronizing light rail systems and buses. In the Austrian city of Graz and in Singapore, public transport has been brought under the management of a single authority in order to reduce such problems. There is a single transferable ticketing system, and timetables and information are coordinated to make life as easy as possible for passengers. As a result of these improvements, use of public transport has accelerated and car use declined in both cities. Such systems are providing valuable lessons for other cities around the world and are now being copied in many locations.

VIEWPOINTS

'The constantly increasing level of road congestion has become a major problem for the whole of industry. It is absolutely vital the [UK] government takes every possible action to improve the operation of the existing road network, as well as making longer term plans for motorway upgrades and widening'
Richard Turner, Chief Executive, Freight Transport Association, UK

'Adding highway capacity to solve traffic congestion is like buying larger pants to deal with your weight problem.'
Michael Replogle, Environmental Defense, USA

VIEWPOINT

'Park & Ride allows commuters, coming into Cambridge, to enjoy stress free travel and beat the queues. It also allows visitors and shoppers to take the direct route to the heart of the city.'
Cambridgeshire County Council website, UK

Changing priorities

Those who campaign for improved transport policies believe that one of the most important tasks is to change transportation priorities. In particular, they argue that private cars should be given lower priority than other forms of transport. Many cities are already adopting such an approach, for instance by marking out dedicated bus lanes. This helps to speed up local bus services, making them more frequent and reliable and so encouraging more people to use them. Bus lanes have been particularly successful when combined with 'park and ride' facilities. These allow people to leave their cars at one of several car parks around the city perimeter and then catch a regular bus service into the centre.

A section of road in Paris, France, is set aside exclusively for buses. Priority lanes such as these can greatly improve the efficiency of public transportation.

Priorities can be assigned in other ways too. In the Netherlands, for example, buses are given priority at traffic lights, thanks to an intelligent traffic control system. In the USA, high occupancy vehicle (HOV) lanes are increasingly common, allowing cars carrying at least two people to use a separate, faster-moving lane. Such measures have encouraged carpooling schemes in cities such as Los Angeles where people meet at parking lots and then share a ride into the city centre using the HOV lane. Many parking lots have lock-up facilities for cyclists so the system is not just for car users. Providing more secure storage for bicycles has been central to the growth in bicycle use in European cities such as Copenhagen, Strasbourg and Freiburg. It is also a very sensible policy as six bicycles can use the road space taken up by a single car and around twenty will fit into a typical car parking space.

Safe storage for bicycles, shown here in Ravenna, Italy, is essential to encouraging their greater use.

Access for all

Of course, any planning changes must ensure that everyone has access to transportation. Policies that ban motorized vehicles from urban centres and pedestrianize main streets can be a problem for the elderly or disabled who may not be very mobile. Planners must ensure that these people continue to have access and that the available transportation meets their needs too. This is especially true of many European societies where the population is ageing rapidly. In Italy, for example, an estimated 35 per cent of the population will be over sixty-five in 2050.

FACT

In a UK government survey, two-thirds of people questioned believed that pedestrians and cyclists should be given priority in towns and cities. Only 1 in 7 disagreed.

The wider picture

Some of the most successful transportation policies have been those where transportation is considered as part of a wider planning process. Curitiba, one of Brazil's fastest-growing cities, is a good example of this. In the city and its suburbs, all new developments are planned in such a way that they are served by the city's highly efficient bus network. A system of feeder buses serves the suburbs and links up with the city centre service which runs on dedicated bus highways to ensure a frequent and regular service. In this way all parts of the city are connected, and almost 70 per cent of the population uses the bus system each day. Central to the success of Curitiba's bus system is a flat-rate fare. This avoids the problems encountered in some other cities where poorer communities living on the city outskirts cannot afford to use public transport. In Manila in the Philippines, for example, poorer residents spend up to 14 per cent of their income on travelling in to the city to work.

This very successful and environment-friendly bus system in Curitiba, Brazil, is now being copied in other cities across South America.

Rethinking land use

In the USA and UK, new developments – such as out-of-town retail or industrial parks, and leisure facilities – are increasingly spreading beyond the city centre. Other countries, including the Netherlands and Japan, have banned such developments. They believe them to be unsustainable because they encourage increased dependency on private motor vehicles and are often poorly connected to existing public transport networks.

Some retailers, such as this furniture store near Birmingham in the UK, have been accused of encouraging greater car use by setting up in out-of-town locations, away from public transport networks.

Instead, in the Netherlands, a land planning system called 'ABC' was introduced in 1990 to encourage development that suits the availability of transportation facilities. 'Group A' locations, for example, are those easily accessible by public transport and are designated for shops and offices where there is a high flow of people. Parking spaces are limited to just 10 per 100 employees to help keep car commuting below 20 per cent. Greater car use is expected in 'group C' locations, but parking spaces are still limited to 40 per 100 employees. Many people believe that this type of innovative urban planning is essential to the future of transportation, but such policies are difficult to enforce unless they have the support of those they are intended to benefit.

DEBATE

Should out-of-town developments, such as retail parks and leisure facilities, be banned in the interests of more sustainable transportation?

CHOICES
AND ACTION

More choice

For some areas and people, there are relatively few transportation choices. Remote rural areas, for example, may have no public transport services at all, while cycling is probably inappropriate for most elderly people. In other regions, people may be unable to afford a private motor vehicle or may not have a driving licence. Because the transportation needs of individuals are so varied, it seems the only way to meet everyone's requirements is to provide them with greater choice.

Sparsely populated regions, like this farming area in Iowa, USA, often suffer from a lack of public transportation services.

This would enable people to select the most appropriate mode of transport for each specific journey. For a small shopping trip to a local shop, walking or cycling might be best, whereas a larger shopping trip could be better planned using the bus or light rail service. Of course some trips will be better suited to a car (if people have access to one), such as visiting relatives in a remote part of the country or travelling late at night when security may be a concern. The same sort of choices also apply to the transportation of freight, with air, rail, boat and road each having particular benefits and drawbacks.

In general, urban areas have greater choice of transportation because their higher population density makes transport systems cheaper to operate. This means that dependence on private cars tends to be lower in more urban areas, as in the table showing transportation patterns in the UK (below).

Old habits die hard

In several countries, including the USA and UK, people continue to rely overwhelmingly on private cars, even when a good choice of alternative transportation exists. This is an extremely wasteful use of transportation resources. For instance, some 60-80 per cent of car journeys are not essential or provide no real benefit over using available public transportation. These figures show that continuing to build a transportation system around the private motor car is not only bad for the environment, congestion and public health, but also a poor use of resources.

A busy bus, train and tram interchange at Freiburg Station in Germany. Densely populated urban centres usually have greater transportation choices than rural areas.

Transportation modes by type and region in the UK, 1999/2001.

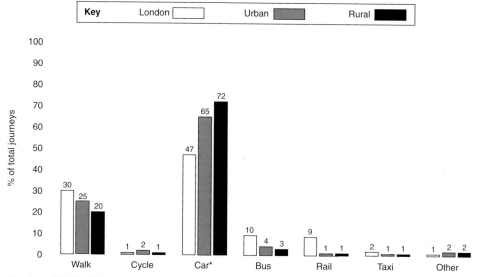

Key   London   Urban   Rural

Based on a UK National Travel survey for urban and rural areas, December 2002.
* Includes travel by car as driver or passenger.

Rising to the challenge

In several European cities, and an increasing number of North American ones, communities have initiated voluntary responses to transportation problems. Car pooling is one example, and it operates in various ways. At the most basic level, people simply combine their journey requirements and share a car trip instead of each driving individually. In US cities, such as Los Angeles, Seattle and New York, car pool schemes (where people park in special lots on the city outskirts and share the final part of their journey into the city) are now common.

More complicated schemes exist in several cities where, instead of owning their own vehicles, people join a car share scheme and book use of a vehicle as and when they need it. This reduces their costs and means they can choose vehicles according to their needs, such as a small car for a local shopping trip or a larger 'people-carrier' for a family day out. They can also choose to use a car for as little as one hour, allowing them to avoid the

weblinks

For more information on the benefits of car pooling, go to www.waylinks.co.uk/series/21debates/transportation

A sign advertises a car sharing scheme in Venice, Italy. Such schemes are growing in popularity in Europe.

expense of traditional car-hire firms which normally charge full-day or half-day rates. Car shares can be small or large. In Berlin, for example, a local neighbourhood scheme shares just three cars among forty neighbours. In contrast, Switzerland (one of the first countries to start car sharing) has some very large schemes such as 'Mobility Car Sharing' which, in early 2003, had 1,770 vehicles serving 400 communities or 49,200 customers.

Road charges, or tolls, are another way of reducing pollution and congestion. Drivers think twice about driving their cars if they have to pay extra to use roads and motorways. This toll barrier is near the popular Spanish tourist resort of Alicante.

New attitudes

The success of initiatives such as car sharing will depend on people adopting new attitudes to transportation. Experts argue that, far from robbing people of their mobility, greater use of public transportation and schemes such as car sharing will actually increase their mobility by removing unnecessary traffic from the roads. In Switzerland, for instance, studies have shown that people using a single shared car can remove the equivalent of around ten private vehicles from the roads. The problem is that many people are reluctant to share journeys with strangers, or to give up their vehicles which they believe give them ultimate freedom and mobility.

FACT

At the beginning of 2003, there were over thirty-six cities in the USA that had started car share schemes.

DEBATE

Should individuals give up their personal vehicles for the good of the environment and the benefit of the communities they live in?

THE FUTURE OF TRANSPORTATION

A balancing act

Getting the future of transportation right will be a tricky balancing act. With some forms of transportation, such as long-haul air travel, there is no realistic alternative because of the time involved in such journeys. However, short-haul flights could be replaced by high-speed rail links which would carry more passengers and have less environmental impact. France's high-speed TGV train between Paris and Lyons led to a 50 per cent fall in air passengers within a month when it was introduced on that route in 1981.

At a more local level, although privately owned cars remain the favoured mode of transport in many countries, evidence suggests that this is not sustainable for the future. Alternatives such as walking and cycling, and public transit systems (including light rail and buses), could provide solutions but will not be taken up until factors such as reliability, frequency and safety are improved. Car-users will need to see real advantages in the alternatives before they are prepared to make the switch.

Technology solutions

Modern technological developments, such as improved fuels and cleaner, more efficient engines, can help to reduce the impact of transportation on the environment, but will not, on their own, solve problems like congestion and traffic accidents. Technology can help fulfil these broader aims, however, by providing people with improved transportation information and making it easier to

FACT

In the UK, Internet shopping more than doubled between December 2001 and December 2002, growing nineteen times faster than sales in the high street.

use various services. In some cities, for example, bus and tram shelters now display live updated information about when the next service is due. The Internet is also being used – for the online booking of car share vehicles or finding travel companions to establish a local car pool.

In some cases, the Internet is being used to avoid journeys altogether. Online shopping, for instance, is growing in popularity around the world. Many supermarkets will now allow people to do their food shopping online and will even deliver it free of charge. In business too, the Internet is used for video-conferencing, allowing meetings to be held without people actually travelling to meet in person. Internet banking also avoids the need to travel to handle financial matters. To date, such options remain limited in many less developed countries. However, as technology costs continue to fall and more people get online, such services may help to reduce transportation demand in the future.

weblinks

For an example of an online shopping service, go to www.waylinks.co.uk/series/21debates/transportation

A teenager in Austin, Texas, uses the Internet for home shopping. Future generations could grow up taking such services for granted and so reduce the need for mobility and transportation.

─ weblinks ─

For more information on European Mobility Week, go to
www.waylinks.co.uk/series/21debates/transportation

Force for change

Some believe that transportation problems can only be solved by direct action from local authorities or national governments. Such actions might include banning private vehicles from city centres, the raising of road or fuel taxes to deter motorists, or the introduction of road charging. Road charging already exists in many cities such as Singapore, where it was introduced in 1998 to reduce the volume of traffic entering the city during rush hour. Other cities are now introducing similar systems. In the UK, for example, motor vehicles wishing to enter central London during the day (between 7am and 6.30pm) have had to pay a £5 daily congestion charge since February 2003.

This scene of congested roads in Los Angeles, USA, is repeated across the world. Do people really want to face a future of endless traffic jams?

THE FUTURE OF TRANSPORTATION

However, forcing change is often unpopular with voters, even where surveys have shown that transportation issues are considered a public priority. People want to see alternatives in place before they are forced to change their current transportation methods. But it is difficult to establish alternatives until there is sufficient demand to make the necessary investment worthwhile.

Personal actions count

Environmentalists and transport campaigners are increasingly focusing on the message that personal actions count. They are encouraging people to reconsider their need for transportation and choose the best option for each specific journey. In the UK, for example, around 25 per cent of journeys are less than 3.2 km (2 miles) and 58 per cent less than 8 km (5 miles) long – distances that could be walked or cycled by the majority of people.

Support for rethinking transportation is certainly growing. Millions of individuals across the world participate in 'car-free' days, for example, and use public transport or walk and cycle instead. Since they began in the late 1990s, car-free days have become major events. In Europe, the event was expanded to become 'European Mobility Week' in 2002, a week-long focus on different forms of transportation, each publicized on its own day. Such events certainly raise awareness of solutions to some of the world's transportation problems, but they are of little use unless those solutions are put into everyday practice. This book has shown that technology and governments may provide some of the answers, but it is ultimately up to individuals like you and me to take the problems personally and make our own transportation choices for the twenty-first century.

VIEWPOINT

'The £5 daily congestion charge will help get London moving. It will reduce traffic, making journeys and delivery times more reliable, and raise millions each week to re-invest in London's transport system.'
Transport for London website

DEBATE

From what you have learned in this book, what would you select as the three most important actions that individuals could take to ensure better transportation in the twenty-first century? What reasons do you have for your choices?

GLOSSARY

acid rain acidic rain produced when pollutants such as sulphur dioxide and nitrogen oxides (emitted when fuels are burned) mix with water vapour in the air to form an acidic solution which falls to the ground. It is damaging to plants, trees, lakes and buildings.

altitude the measured height of an object (e.g. aircraft) or location (e.g. mountain) above sea level. Normally measured in metres or feet.

biodiesel a motor fuel made from plant extracts that is used in a pure form or mixed with conventional diesel fuel. Biodiesel is cleaner than standard diesel fuels.

boat-plane a form of aircraft that has an underside similar to a boat's hull which allows it to take off and land on water.

budget airline an airline company that specializes in low-cost air travel. Such flights are normally on short routes between major cities.

car pool a system in which people share the use of motor cars in order to reduce the number of vehicles on the road, share costs and limit the environmental impact of motor vehicle emissions.

car sharing a scheme in which people share the costs and use of communal vehicles rather than having their own. Members of a car sharing scheme only pay for the distance and/or time that they actually use a vehicle.

climate change the process of long-term changes to the world's climate (e.g. warming or cooling). This occurs naturally, but is today occurring as a result of human activities polluting the atmosphere.

commute regular travel to work, usually from a suburb to a city.

congestion where vehicles overcrowd a street or road making movement difficult or impossible for some time. Sometimes called 'traffic jams'.

containerization the packaging of goods and freight into standard-sized containers which can then be easily transported by road, rail or sea and transferred between different types of transport.

courier somebody who delivers important or urgent packages by hand. A bicycle or motor vehicle is normally used for transportation.

cycle lock-up a storage facility for the safe keeping of bicycles while they are not in use. They are often found at people's places of work or in public places such as railway stations.

deforestation the removal of trees, shrubs and forest vegetation. This can be natural (due to forest fires, typhoons, etc) or a result of human action (logging, ranching, construction, land clearance, etc).

developed countries the wealthier countries of the world including Europe, North America, Japan and Australia and New Zealand. People living there are normally healthy, well educated and work in a wide variety of high-technology industries.

e-bicycle a bicycle that is fitted with an electric (normally battery-powered) motor to assist the rider and reduce the need for them to pedal.

emissions polluting waste products (normally gas and solid particles) released into the atmosphere. These include carbon, sulphur and lead from car exhaust fumes.

erosion a process whereby something becomes worn (eroded). For example, the removal of material (soil or rock) by the forces of nature (wind or rain) or people (deforestation, vehicle tracks, etc).

fossil fuels fuels from the fossilized remains of plants and animals formed over millions of years. They include coal, oil and natural gas. Once used, they are gone – non-renewable.

freight goods carried by commercial vehicles, sometimes also known as cargo.

fuel tax a tax (charge) on the purchase of fuel. Such taxes can be used to change fuel consumption patterns.

global warming the gradual warming of the Earth's atmosphere as a result of greenhouse gases, such as carbon dioxide and methane, trapping heat. Human activity has increased the level of these gases in the atmosphere.

gridlock situation whereby congestion affects a wider area than usual so that vehicles are unable to move in any direction at all.

heavy goods vehicle (HGV) normally a tractor and trailer unit for transporting heavy goods by road, but more generally used to describe any goods vehicle weighing 7.5 tonnes or more.

high occupancy vehicle (HOV) a vehicle carrying at least two (sometimes defined as three) passengers.

home zone an area in which traffic is limited or banned in order to create safer and more enjoyable streets for the people living there.

hull the main body of a ship or aeroplane.

GLOSSARY

hydrogen fuel an alternative fuel currently being developed that releases no pollutants. It is made by combining hydrogen and oxygen in a special fuel cell.

infrastructure networks that enable communication and/or people, transport and the economy to function, such as roads, railways, electricity and phone lines, and pipelines carrying oil or water.

innovative new and original. Using roadrailers (see below), for example, is an innovative way to encourage greater integration of road and rail transportation.

intercity transport which connects two or more cities.

light railway relatively small-scale (sometimes driverless) railways that run on sunken or elevated tracks, providing a quick, efficient and less polluting means of transport. They are increasingly popular in busy city centres such as London (UK) and Bangkok (Thailand).

mass transit movement of large numbers of people.

metro a railway system in a town or city which runs either wholly or partly underground.

mobility the ability to move from one location to another, e.g. for leisure or work.

motorized transport any form of transport which has a motor fitted to it, but usually restricted to mean road vehicles, e.g. cars, lorries, buses and motorcycles.

non-renewable resources those that, once used, are gone and cannot be replaced, except over millions of years. These include coal, oil and natural gas.

park and ride scheme a scheme whereby cars are parked in out-of-town car parks and drivers travel into urban centres on buses or trams, so reducing congestion and pollution.

public transit system a transportation system, such as a bus or metro network, that is designed to meet the mobility needs of the public.

public transport a network of passenger vehicles, e.g. buses, trains and trams, running on set routes, at set times and fares.

regenerate (a town centre) a process designed to bring new growth to an area following a period of decline. Such plans often involve improved transportation to make the area more attractive to businesses and shoppers.

road pricing policy whereby motorists have to pay to use a particular road or section of road.

roadrailer a road trailer that has been adapted to ride directly on rail lines by using an extra set of steel wheels and retracting its road wheels.

seat-kilometre the movement of one seat space (on an aircraft, for example) over a distance of 1 kilometre. If an aircraft has 100 seats and travels 100 kilometres then it has completed 10,000 seat kilometres (100 x 100 = 10,000).

short-haul flight flights to destinations which are a relatively short distance away.

smog a mixture of fog, smoke and air-borne pollutants such as exhaust fumes.

suburb a district, normally dominated by residential homes, located on the outskirts of a major urban centre.

subway a railway system in a town or city which runs either wholly or partly underground.

sustainable transportation alternative transport systems that meet the needs of today's global population without causing harm to people or the environment, now or in the future.

synchronize (different transport systems) to coordinate timetables so that different transport services connect with each other. Synchronizing a long-distance train with local train or bus services, for example, would mean that passengers did not have to wait for long periods in between journeys.

traffic calming a set of measures designed to slow the flow of road traffic in order to make roads safer for cyclists and pedestrians.

traffic control system a system (normally computerized) that is designed to control the flow of traffic. Such systems can be used to give priority to public transport such as buses and trams.

tram a passenger coach that runs on metal rails sunken into existing roads or on special tramways. Trams are normally powered by electricity from overhead cables. Known as streetcars in the USA.

urban sprawl the process by which new urban development (e.g. housing, leisure and retail complexes) spreads beyond existing town or city boundaries onto surrounding land.

zero emission vehicle a vehicle, such as a bicycle, that does not release any polluting waste products.

BOOKS TO READ

Sustainable World: Transport
Rob Bowden
(Hodder Wayland, 2003)

Children's Encyclopedia of Transport:
On the Move
Andrew Nahum
(Marshall Editions, 2001)

Earth Alert!: Transport
Andrew Church and Amanda Church
(Hodder Wayland, 2001)

Environment Starts Here!: Transport
Angela Royston
(Hodder Wayland, 2001)

Earth in Danger: Transport
Polly Goodman
(Hodder Wayland, 2001)

Great Inventions: Transport
Paul Dowswell
(Heinemann Library, 2002)

A Century of Change: Transport
Jane Shuter
(Heinemann Library, 1999)

USEFUL ADDRESSES

Friends of the Earth UK
26-28 Underwood Street
London N1 7JQ
UK
Tel: 0207 490 1555

Friends of the Earth USA
1025 Vermont Ave. NW,
3rd Floor
Washington DC
20005-6303
USA
Tel: 1 202 783 7400

Sustrans (UK)
35 King Street
Bristol BS1 4DZ
UK
Tel: 0117 926 8893

Institute for Transportation and
Development Policy (ITDP)
115 West 30th Street (12th Floor)
New York, NY, 10001, Suite 1205
USA
Tel: 1 212 629 8001

The Centre for Alternative and Sustainable
Transport (CAST)
School of Sciences
Mellor Building
College Road
Stoke-on-Trent
Staffordshire ST4 2DE
UK
Tel: 01782 295771

For additional topics that are relevant to this book go to
www.waylinks.co.uk/series/21debates/transportation

INDEX

Numbers in **bold** refer to illustrations.

INDEX